pray the Word

31 Prayers That Touch *the* Heart *of* God

TIECE L. KING

PRAYERSHOP PUBLISHING

TERRE HAUTE, INDIANA

PrayerShop Publishing is the publishing arm of Harvest Prayer Ministries and the Church Prayer Leaders Network. Harvest Prayer Ministries exists to transform lives through teaching prayer. Its online prayer store, www.prayershop.org, has more than 500 prayer resources available for purchase.

ISBN: 978-1-935012-50-4

This resource contains Scripture-based prayers. Each prayer is filled with thoughts based on these verses. Only short phrases appear that are taken from various versions. That is why we do not cite a particular version.

1 2 3 4 5 | 2018 2017 2016 2015 2014

Dedication

In loving memory of my mother, Kay Bassett,

who without realizing it,

discipled me in prayer in the watches of the night,

through the crack in her bedroom door.

Acknowledgments

No life is formed in a vacuum. My life like yours, has been shaped through experiences and observations. The signature of Jesus has been imprinted indelibly upon me by many: a father who loved me unconditionally, a mother of desperate faith, intentional Sunday School teachers, passionate youth pastors, prayer mentors encountered in the pages of many books, missionary co-workers, dear friends on the pilgrimage—brave enough to dialogue about faith, to press into the mystery of prayer, and to wrestle through both the presence and absence of the power of God.

So with deep gratitude for these investments in me, I want to thank especially:

my heavenly Father, for loving me as His daughter, disciplining me for my good and allowing me to experience suffering that I might learn to cling to Him.

my husband David, for his encouragement in all things and his determination to stay upon the "road less traveled" and take me with him.

Mr. Jeff Reitz who stepped into my life at the age of twelve when my father died, and has faithfully pointed me to Jesus ever since.

the communities of faith called York Alliance Church and the Evangelical Church of Bangkok, who chose to follow me as I followed Jesus into a life of deeper prayer.

Dr. Martin Sanders (Alliance Theological Seminary) for asking me the hard questions at God-appointed times.

Jon Graf at Harvest Prayer who believed with me and for me that a book was possible and useful for the kingdom.

and all of the loving co-laborers who translated, formatted and edited parts of this work into multiple languages. Siree Chanyaputhipong, Somluck Ruengkasab, Lisa Lehman, Boonravee Sirilert, I hsuan Liu, Karen Tan, Juana Martinez, Ann Searing, Marie Maldonado, Sri Kosen, Catherine Harsono, Priskila Paksoal, Janine Rembas, Kinue Onishi, Hiromi Koshy, Dawn Mekunwattana, Kevin Moua—eternity will reveal the impact of your sacrificial gift of time and skill!

Foreword

Prayer. Simplicity. Each word may conjure up a variety of nuanced impressions, thoughts and ideas—some negative, most positive. As spiritual disciplines however they are critically invaluable. In my study of spiritual disciplines, I have noticed that some *single* disciplines when combined in practice become more than doubly fruitful in the lives of Christ-followers.

Take for instance the disciplines of solitude and silence. When practiced singularly, they have great impetus for driving the distracted heart back to its Center, its Maker. To be alone with the Master. Or to listen and not speak in His Presence. Yet how many hearts have found the spiritual heat turned up when we sequester ourselves *so that* we can listen more carefully and actually hear even more clearly?

The book you hold is a powerful combination of at least two of the classical disciplines—prayer and simplicity. Tiece King offers us the chance to move away from the flood of methodology for a better prayer life and instead, very simply and clearly, embrace an "ancient future." We are invited to return to the "prayer primer" of the very first God-followers: the very Word of God. Tiece takes the words of Scripture and assists us, not merely in the recitation of them, but in the application of them to the depths of our hearts and the circumstances of our daily lives. If we allow it, this tool is the Word of God to us, in us and through us. You will find that your heart will change as you make these daily prayers your own.

It has been a refreshing experience to witness the development of this simple prayer tool. Over a span of 20 years, the daily prayers have been "road-tested" in the local church. After creating and collating the prayers for this book-tool, Tiece employed a number of fellow pilgrims to proofread and review the work. To a person, unsolicited, each individual expressed in their own personal way, that in their review, they felt as though they had spent time with Jesus. That was of course, well beyond encouraging, for it is the very intent of this prayer book and indeed, prayer in general. Not by supplication in our own words to "get our way with God" but through praying God's Word to be with Jesus, aligning our hearts with our Master's heart.

Tiece King is one of the finest pastors I know. I know this because she has, for the past 20 years, been teaching churches to pray. And because I cleverly convinced her to marry me over 30 years ago, I have not only pastored alongside her in these churches, but I have learned personally (and continue to learn), how to pray simply and deeply. In this book, using the words of the "great Shepherd of the sheep," she pastors us into the presence of the One who hears our prayers and the hearts that pray them. I encourage you to make use of this tool and the opportunity to simply and prayerfully "be still and know" once again, or even for the first time.

–David R. King, Lead Pastor,
Evangelical Church of Bangkok

Introduction

In shaping us into the image of Christ, God often takes us to harrowing places which turn our lives upside down and inside out. Places that make our knees shake and rob us of our appetites; places of soul anguish, wrestling, and miraculous intervention; places of the strengthening of our faith *and* ultimately, incredible victory. It is through prayer that we see desert places become springs of water and dead things come to life! And as we allow the Word of God to frame and align our praying, our faith increases in order to believe God for even greater things, our minds are transformed and renewed, and the living out of our faith becomes infused with new life as we agree with, claim, and proclaim the Word of God in prayer!

The prayers in the pages of this book were born out of life experiences and a longing for more of Jesus in my own life and in His Church. God in His mercy took me to a place of ultimate desperation for Him, where "safe praying" was no longer an option and my only solace was His Word.

These prayers are intended to help us in agreeing with the Word of God for the things of God, beginning with the removal of obstacles in our own hearts in order to make way for the work of the Holy Spirit. They are meant to be prayed from your heart, not read with your mind, to be read slowly, savored, interacted with. There are places within the body of many of the prayers to pause and consider, to listen for the whisper of the Holy Spirit and to respond to His nudge, to interject petitional requests, or simply to be still. I encourage you not to hurry through, but determine to make space for your heart to engage as you pray.

The Scripture references at the bottom of each prayer are those which are referenced within the body of the prayer. For further meditation, look these up and read them for yourself. I admonish you to choose at the outset to humble yourself in the presence of the Holy Spirit and submit to the authority of the Word of God. It is active and powerful and its application to our lives through prayer is transformational!

In all things, not just the prayers of this book, the Word of God must be our foundation. As we learn to pray it into our lives and pray it back to our loving heavenly Father, we will be forever changed. As faith increases and rises up within us because of this transformational savoring of the Word, the situations and circumstances around us will be impacted, and the Church for which Jesus died will be revived!

May it be so, Lord Jesus!

–Tiece L. King

Your Love Endures Forever

Consider praying this prayer out loud as a declaration of praise . . .

I will give thanks to You, O Lord, and call on Your name. I will make known among the nations—in this nation—the amazing things that You have done. I will sing to You and praise You alone. Teach me what it means to "glory in Your name" that my heart might always rejoice in You. For it is my great desire to seek Your face always and remember the wonders that You have done.

I give thanks to You, Lord, for You are good. Your love endures forever!

You remembered me when I was lost and without You and freed me from the enemy! Your love endures forever!

While I was still in my sin, Christ died for me! Hallelujah! Your love endures forever!

You have not kept a record of my sin, or treat me as my sin deserves, but through Christ You have removed my sin from me as far as the east is from the west and remember it no more! Hallelujah! Your faithful love endures forever!

I will bless Your name, O Lord, and in Your name I will lift up my hands, for Your faithful love endures forever!

I will praise You, O Lord, there is no God like You in heaven or on earth—You who keep Your covenant of love with Your servants who continue wholeheartedly in Your way. There is nothing too difficult for You! Your love endures forever!

Yours is the greatness O Lord and the power and the glory and the majesty and the splendor, for everything in heaven and earth is Yours.

You are exalted as head over all. Wealth and honor come from You alone for You are the ruler of all things. In Your hands are strength and power to exalt and give strength to all. And I join with all of heaven, and Your people everywhere in giving You thanks and praising Your glorious name! Hallelujah! Your faithful love endures forever! Hallelujah! Hallelujah! Amen and Amen!

Psalm 105:1-5; Psalm 136:1-9,23-24; Romans 5:6; Psalm 103:10-12;
Psalm 63:4; 2 Chronicles 6:14; 1 Chronicles 29:10-13

DAY TWO

Save Me from Myself, O Lord

Quiet your heart before you begin. Be still and know that He is God (Psalm 46:10).

Father, thank You for the promise of Your Word that as I come near to You, You will come near to me. Thank You for the blessing that is mine as I seek hard after You. But I come to You, heavenly Father, confessing that I have allowed other loves to stand in the way of my relationship with You. I have often come near to You with my mouth and have said the right words, and yet my heart has remained distant from You, hard and untouched by Your Spirit. Help me Father! Be merciful to me, for I long to be one who seeks You with all of my heart and finds You.

May I not draw near to You and then retreat again to lesser loves. Save me from myself, I pray—from self-righteousness, self-provision, and selfishness. Strengthen me to remain in You, to learn to abide in You, so that I can bear spiritual fruit, for I know that I can do nothing unless I am abiding in Christ Jesus.

Empower me by Your Spirit to earnestly seek You. May my longing to draw near to You be reflected in my thought life what I allow myself to read and see; the music I listen to; the conversations I engage in; how I conduct myself in my home, neighborhood, or work; and when I think no one is watching. In all of these things and so many more teach me what it means to live and move and have my very being in You alone. I invite You, Holy Spirit, to break up the unplowed ground of my heart, that it might become a fertile field in which Your Word can grow. Soften my heart again, I pray, that I might more clearly hear Your voice and walk in Your ways. In Jesus' name. Amen.

James 4:8; Psalm 34:10; Isaiah 29:13; Jeremiah 29:13; John 15:4, 5; Hebrews 11:6; Acts 17:28; Jeremiah 4:3: Matthew 13:18-23

Walk as Jesus Walked

I thank You, Father, for the example of the life of Jesus. Help me to follow in His steps, for I know that whoever truly follows Him will not walk in darkness but will have the light of life. Forgive me Father for the times I have chosen darkness over the light of Your presence. Help me to love You above all others and all other things. May I listen to Your voice, be known by You, and follow You. May I not be a stumbling block in anyone's path or be discredited as Your disciple this day because of my words or actions for You have said in Your Word that whoever claims to live in Jesus must walk as He did!

May I become a disciple who, like the Apostle Paul, can say to others without boasting, "Follow my example, as I follow the example of Christ!" Empower me by Your Spirit to be an example of Jesus in my home, place of work, neighborhood, or school. May my encounters with friends and strangers alike be seasoned with the presence of Christ. May I fix my thoughts and my eyes on Him. In everything, may I set an example by doing what is good. Even in the face of suffering, may I be an example of patience. And Father, I ask that You would give me opportunity to entrust to someone else all that You are teaching and showing me, that I might truly become a disciple who makes disciples.

As one who follows You, Lord, may I continue in faith and stand firm, never moving from the hope held out to me in the gospel. Remind me that as Your disciple I have been called to the ministry and message of reconciliation as Christ's ambassador. May I be a worthy vessel through whom You can implore others to be reconciled to Christ, that lasting spiritual fruit may be born out of my life. All this I ask in the mighty name of Jesus. Amen.

---

1 Peter 2:21; John 8:12; Luke 14:26; 1 John 2:5; John 10:27; 2 Corinthians 6:3; 1 Corinthians 11:1; Hebrews 12:2; Titus 2:7; James 5:10; 2 Timothy 2:2; Matthew 28:19; Colossians 1:23; 2 Corinthians 5:18-20; John 15:16

DAY FOUR

I Will Remember

Father, You are great and worthy of all my praise! How awesome are the things You have done! I am grateful and I bless Your holy name, Lord, for I have seen You at work on my behalf again and again, and I worship You, for only You could do these mighty things. You alone are God.

Thank You for Your provision. I remember when . . . (*add from own life*)

Thank You for Your protection. I remember when . . .

I remember the day you saved me . . . and I thank You for shining the light of Your presence into my darkness and not treating me as my sin deserves! (*Pause and remember and give thanks.*)

Teach me by Your Spirit to live with Your praise always on my lips. Forgive my ungratefulness, I pray, and change my complaining heart! When I look back and remember how You have been with me, how Your hand has been on me, I am filled with gratitude and praise. But too easily I am captured again by the storms around me and lose sight of You and my faith seems to disappear. Yet, O Lord, You have been faithful, faithful to all Your promises. Therefore, I will not fear, even though everything around me seems to give way and I seem to lose my footing in the midst of changing times. Regardless of the storms I face, my hope is in You, Lord, and Your unfailing love for me.

I ask, Father, that You write new songs of worship on my heart for You are worthy. Give me an undivided heart that I may fear Your name and honor You. As I remember all that you have done in the past, increase my faith Lord and my trust in You for those things that loom before me today. Help me in my weakness. Remove the shadows of doubt that still linger and affect my life. May all that I am and all that I do flow out of a heart of worship and adoration for You. For You are glorious, and I put my hope in You alone.

Psalm 145:3; Psalm 66:1; Psalm 103:10; Psalm 34:1; Psalm 103:2; Psalm 33:4; Psalm 46:1-2; Psalm 147:11; Psalm 86:11; Mark 9:24; Psalm 29:1-2

Praise Him in the Storm

Father, I confess that I do not know what to do, but my eyes are upon You. How thankful I am for the promise of Your Word that when I grieve, You give me a crown of beauty, that even when I mourn there is gladness found in You. And when I despair and feel hopeless in my circumstances, as I look to You, You will cloak me in a garment of praise.

My desire, Father, is to always praise You, but I confess that often, like Peter, I look away from the face of Jesus, see the fierceness of the storm around me, sink into my circumstances, and lose all ability to believe that You will fight my battles. Why is my faith so small? Why do I doubt? Forgive me Father and have mercy on me. Help me, I pray! Destroy doubt in my life and make it true of me that though the fig tree does not bud (my dreams do not come to fruition . . .) and there are no grapes on the vines (my burdens seem endless . . .), though the olive crop fails and the fields produce no food (my financial resources are sadly lacking . . .) though there are no sheep in the pen or cattle in the stalls (my worldly possessions are minimal at best . . .), may I still be joyful and praise Your name—for You are my God and my Savior (I have Jesus!). You are my strength, and you enable me to rise above the circumstances of my life and the cares of this world.

May I follow the example of King Jehoshaphat and the army of Israel and sing and praise Your name and leave the battles of my life in Your hands. Even in the most overwhelming situations may I choose to give thanks to You, rejoice in You, knowing that Your love endures forever. I choose this day to praise You regardless of what I see with my earthly eyes, and I rejoice that my name is written in heaven because of the finished work of Jesus on the cross. Thank You that the victory is sure. In Jesus' name. Amen.

---

2 Chronicles 20:12; Isaiah 61:3; Matthew 14:25-33; Habakkuk 3:17;
2 Chronicles 20:21, 22; Psalm 5:11; Luke 10:20

DAY SIX

I Choose to Wait on You

Father, help me to be confident that I will see Your goodness in the land of the living. Help me to wait for You, to be strong and take heart and to wait. I ask that my life would increasingly become a proclamation of Your greatness and goodness. Make me fearless in the face of trials. Strengthen me, I pray, to stand firm and release my lips to worship You—You are great and awesome O God! You alone are God, creator of heaven and earth, and I join with all creation and praise Your holy name! Holy! Holy! Holy! Lord God Almighty, who always has been, who is here right now, and who is coming!

Forgive me for withholding my praise and adoration, for being silent and even sullen and losing sight of Your greatness and glory. In doing so I've allowed You to become small in my eyes and have taken situations and concerns into my own hands instead of trusting You. You have said that the one who trusts in man and depends on the arm of flesh for his strength is cursed. Father, forgive me for the ways that I have trusted in others or my own strength instead of trusting You. Increase my faith, Lord. May I become like a tree planted by the water that doesn't fear when heat comes, but whose leaves are always green.

15

I choose now to cast my cares on You . . .
relationships in my life that are fractured,
those who are close to me who have yet to call on Your name,
the weariness of finances,
the brokenness of the world . . .

O Lord, increase my faith! Enable me by Your Spirit to speak Your word with great boldness into every situation of my life, regardless of what is happening around me. I choose again to put my trust in You and hope in Your unfailing love, for You are my strength and those who hope in You will not be disappointed. Thank You that You are at work on my behalf, and nothing is too difficult for You. Nothing! In Jesus' name. Amen.

Psalm 27:13; Acts 4:23-31; Isaiah 6:3; Jeremiah 17:5, 7-8; Psalm 55:22; Acts 4:29; Habakkuk 3:17-19; Isaiah 49:23; Luke 1:37

DAY SEVEN

You Are Doing Great Things

Give voice to your praise by reading the following prayer out loud.

Praise the Lord, O my soul! Praise Your Holy Name. Praise the Lord, O my soul, I will not forget all the things You have done! You forgive all my sins (Hallelujah!) and heal all my diseases. You have redeemed my life from the pit—from sin, darkness and destruction, and crowned me with love and compassion. You satisfy my desires with good things, so that my youth is renewed like the eagle's. You are compassionate and gracious, O Lord, slow to anger, and abounding in love. You do not treat me as my sin deserves or repay me according to my iniquities! (Hallelujah! Praise Your holy name!) I praise You Lord! My soul cries out, "Great are You Lord! How awesome are Your deeds!" Praise the Lord! Praise the Lord! I praise You, O God, for what You are doing among Your people—Your Church—for we are the sheep of Your pasture! You are turning our hearts of stone into hearts of flesh, by Your Spirit. You are restoring to us the joy of our salvation. Yes! Joy and gladness are being restored to Your people, and I praise Your name! Only You can do these things! You are releasing the tongues of your people to sing of your righteousness and declare Your praise! You are renewing our hearts of worship! I praise Your name O God! You are teaching us to love what You love, You are changing us. You are changing me. I praise Your name, for only You can do these great things! Only You can breathe the life of Your Spirit into the dead places of our hearts! Only You can revive and transform Your church!

Father, I will praise You in the presence of Your people! I will lift up my hands in the sanctuary and bless Your great Name. I will declare among Your people that "Your love endures forever!" I will not be kept silent in proclaiming Your greatness and giving You glory. This day, Father, may I be found faithfully praising You in word and deed, heart songs and meditations and acts of love and service. May all that I do and say be a reflection of my love for You, that Jesus may be exalted in and through my life. For Your name and renown are the desire of my heart! In Jesus' name. Amen.

Psalm 103; Psalm 66:3; Psalm 100:3; Ezekiel 11:19; Psalm 51:12-15; Ezekiel 37:3-5; Psalm 134:2; Psalm 136:1; Luke 19:40; Psalm 29:1-2; Isaiah 26:8

DAY EIGHT

Overcomer

Father, Your Word says that I am an overcomer because of the blood of the Lamb, the Lord Jesus Christ, and the word of my testimony—that in Jesus, all the fullness of the Deity lives in bodily form, and I have been given fullness in Christ and share in His authority over every spiritual power and authority! But I confess that I do not feel like an overcomer, and I often give in to the influence of this world instead of submitting to Christ.

O God, save me from myself! May I be full of Your Spirit and Your mighty power—the power of the resurrection! Teach me and use me, that I might be one who sees strongholds demolished in my life and help others to walk in freedom. Thank You, Father, that because I belong to You in Christ Jesus, You surround me with Your presence—that You are a wall of fire around me. You, O Lord, are my refuge and my strength. In every situation and struggle, You are with me. I will not be afraid for my trust is in Your name.

Like Joshua, may I be confident that You are with me and will never leave or forsake me. By Your Spirit at work in me make me to be strong and courageous, to not be afraid or discouraged, but always mindful that You are with me wherever I go. Use me to take back ground that the enemy has stolen. Help me to be self-controlled and alert, knowing that the enemy of my soul is prowling, looking for an opportune moment.

In Jesus' name, strengthen me to submit to You, resist the enemy, and to stand firm in my faith! Give me, I pray, Your perspective of the situations I face and may I live victoriously, as a conqueror, because of Jesus and His love for me. May I be full of faith and Your Word, for I belong to You, Lord Jesus, and You have overcome the world!

Revelation 12:11; Colossians 2:9-10; Ephesians 6:10; Philippians 3:10;
2 Corinthians 10:4; Psalm 125:2; Zechariah 2:5; Psalm 46:1-2; Psalm 20:7;
Joshua 1:5, 9; 1 Peter 5:8-9; Romans 8:37; 1 John 5:4

DAY NINE

I Will Not Fear

As you pray, in the midst of whatever trial you presently find yourself, choose to worship God for who He is.

Father, how desperately I need Your help in aligning my heart with the truth of Your Word. With my mouth I would say that You are in the midst of the difficulties of my life, working them together for my good, but the unease in my heart says otherwise. Help me, O God! By the power of Your Spirit at work in me, change my heart! Remove fear and make me fearless. Remove timidity and make me bold for Your kingdom. Remove doubt and unbelief and increase my faith. For I will remember Your deeds Lord, the miracles that You have done in my life as I have journeyed toward You. I will meditate on all of Your works and think about the many mighty things You have done for me. I purpose this day to worship You alone. I will bow to no other god.

Because You are my God, my refuge and strength, I will not fear even though trouble may seem to surround me. Because of Your great love for me, I know that You will rescue me. You will protect me, be with me, deliver me. Because You are my God, and You have redeemed me and called me by name,

> You will be with me when I pass through the waters of adversity—I will not drown.
>
> The swift current of the trial of disappointment that I find myself in—will not sweep me away.
>
> The fiery trial of sickness or loneliness or financial instability or . . . —will not set me ablaze!

For You are the LORD my God, the Holy One of Israel, my Savior. Therefore, I will praise You, O LORD, with all my heart. I will tell of all Your wonders. I will be glad and rejoice in You and sing praise to Your name. For my hope is in Your unfailing love that is at work on my behalf, for my good, to make me more like Jesus. Seal this work to my heart, I pray. In the beautiful name of the One who died to make me Yours, Jesus. Amen.

Romans 8:28; Isaiah 29:13; Isaiah 41:10; 2 Timothy 1:7; Mark 9:24; Psalm 77:10-15; Daniel 3:16-18; Psalm 91:14-15; Isaiah 41:1-3; Psalm 9:1-2; Psalm 33:18; Romans 8:28

DAY TEN

Remove Every Obstacle

Father, I long for the day when the desert and parched lands of my life will be glad and the wilderness areas yet untouched by Your Spirit will rejoice and blossom!

Open my blind eyes, I pray, and help me to see every area of

my life that has yet to submit to the lordship of Jesus . . .
(*Show me these things as I wait on You.*)
Open my ears, Father, that I might hear and understand
Your Word and the voice of Your Spirit . . . (*Quiet my
noisy mind as I wait on You.*)
Tenderize my heart that I might respond in brokenness and
repentance . . . (*Give me, I pray, the gift of tears as a sign
that You are softening the hard places of my heart.*)

May the Holy Spirit flow from my life and cause every desert place
to become a stream of living water! Have mercy on me, O God! In
Your great compassion, wash away all of my sin and cleanse me. Create
in me a pure, clean heart and renew a steadfast determination within
me to follow hard after You. Restore to me the joy I knew when I first
found You and give me, I pray, a willingness to do Your will. Father, I
ask this that I might become one who You use to walk alongside those
who are still lost in their sin. Make me bold, Father, and may Your
praise always be on my lips. Restore me, and may Your face shine on
me, for I long for more of You. I know of the awesome things that You
have done in the past, but I ask that You renew them in my day! In my
lifetime, make them known!

Your Word promises that You will revive the spirit of the lowly and
the heart of the contrite, and so I choose to humble myself before You.
Teach me and show me what this means, what it looks like in my daily
living. Destroy every area of pride in me, Father, until the humility of
Jesus, His love and compassion, flows from my life like a mighty river.

For the sake of Your Church and a dying world, revive me again
and again! In Jesus' holy name. Amen.

Isaiah 35:1-6; Psalm 51:1-2, 10-15; Psalm 80:7; Habakkuk 3:2; Isaiah 57:14-15

Help Me to Persevere

Quiet your heart before the Lord. Commit to Him those situations in your life that are difficult.

Lord Jesus, You said that in this world I will have trouble, but that I should take heart, for You have overcome the world! Hallelujah Lord! You are greater than all of my fears. You are more powerful than all the powers of darkness that wage war against my soul, O God! You alone are God! May Your name be great and proclaimed loudly in and through my life!

Forgive me Lord, for the times that I do lose heart, and I am overcome by the world. Instead, Father, give me eyes to see that my momentary troubles are achieving for me an eternal glory that will far outweigh them all! And may I be found worshipping You in the midst of the obstacles, challenges, and trials of this life. Remind me constantly, by Your Spirit, that I am not home yet. Empower me to persevere and endure hardships in my life for the sake of Your name and the formation of Your character in me.

I acknowledge that You know all my ways, and that You will bring me through the storms in my life, refining me as gold. May the trials I face teach me to obey Your Word and may my faith be proved genuine and result in praise, glory, and honor to You, Jesus. I confess that You alone are God, there is no other, and I trust in Your name alone to save me. I rest in Your sovereignty and hope in Your name as I wait for You. For You have searched me and You know me and everything about me— when I am still, when I am busy, where I go, and what I do, You know all my ways and every thought I have. Even before I speak a single word, You know it. There isn't anyplace that I can go where You are not there.

Thank You, Father, that even the darkness that seems to engulf me at times is as light to You. I praise You and acknowledge that every day of my life was ordained for me by You. Therefore I submit myself to You alone and stand against the schemes of the enemy in Jesus' name. Amen.

John 16:33; 2 Corinthians 4:17; Revelation 2:3; 1 Peter 1:7; Isaiah 44:6; Psalm 20:7; Psalm 139:1-16; James 4:7

DAY TWELVE

A Living Sacrifice

Father, I thank You for Your great mercy and love poured out for me through the work of Christ. But I confess that I often live without any thought of Your great sacrifice and have engaged my mind and body in things of this world that are not holy or pleasing to You. You have said that presenting my body as a living sacrifice is part of my spiritual worship, and I have forsaken it.

Father, I confess that I have allowed my mind to be entangled with the patterns of this world and its standard instead of the standard of Your Word. Forgive me, Lord! Strengthen me. Be the filter over my eyes and mind.

I have been undisciplined in the care of my physical body and careless about my health and habits. Help me to discipline my body and put to death my fleshly nature. Forgive me Father.

Forgive me for wanting my pursuit of You to be easy. Forgive my slothfulness, O God! May I run after You in such a way as to get the prize and discipline myself so as not to be disqualified.

Give me the gift of wisdom and discernment, I pray, and guard my mind from hollow and deceptive philosophies that depend on human tradition and principles of this world, rather than on Christ and Your Word. I ask this so that my mind might be truly renewed and the way I live transformed. This day, I confess my great desire to follow You alone.

I long, Lord Jesus, to experience Holy Spirit-ignited, transformational living—daily! To see Jesus lived out in me—through me—in ways I have not yet known; grant this, I pray. O Holy Spirit of God, purify me, refine me, I pray, until all of me is conformed to You, Lord Jesus, and I learn the secret and discipline of becoming a living sacrifice. Only You can accomplish this, and I pray in Your great name—in Jesus' name—that it will be so. Amen.

Romans 5:5; Romans 12:1; 1 Corinthians 9:24-27; Colossians 2:8; Romans 8:29

DAY THIRTEEN

Holy Spirit Rain Down

Father, thank You for sending the Counselor, the Holy Spirit, to teach me and remind me of the things that Jesus said. Thank You for His presence with me—forever. Forgive me, Father, for the times that I resist the Holy Spirit, even though I know that He is the One who convicts of sin and righteousness and judgment. How thankful I am that the Holy Spirit helps me in my weakness—that when I don't know what or how I should pray, He intercedes for me in accordance with Your will.

Father, tenderize my heart and make me sensitive to the promptings of the Holy Spirit. I ask that You remove any hardness of heart that still remains in me, and give me a heart of flesh. By Your Spirit, reveal even the hidden sin in my life as I wait on You . . . (*Pause and wait before the Lord, confess those things He brings to your mind.*)

Your Word promises that You, heavenly Father, will give the Holy Spirit to those who ask You, and so I ask, Father, as Your child, fill me afresh with Your Holy Spirit! (*Pause and wait before the Lord, personalize this prayer and make it your own.*)

Empower me by Your Spirit to live victoriously for Christ, that as I am *in* the world, I may not ever be *of* the world. I ask that the power of the Holy Spirit come on me that I might be a witness for You and boldly speak Your Word. Teach me by the Spirit when and what I should say. I long for the fruit of the Spirit to be evident in my life in ever-increasing measure, and to truly walk in the Spirit, so that the desires and passions of my sinful nature are destroyed. Strengthen me by Your Spirit to stand firm against the enemy and to persevere and do Your will. Like the early disciples, may my life be characterized by fullness of joy and the presence of the Holy Spirit, so that Jesus will be seen more clearly in me and through me and my life will bring glory to His name, for this is the longing of my heart. Holy Spirit rain down on me. In Jesus' name I ask these things. Amen.

John 14:26; John 16:8; Romans 8:26-27; Ezekiel 36:26; Luke 11:13; Acts 1:8; Luke 12:12; Galatians 5:22-25; Ephesians 6:11; Acts 13:52

Renew My Mind

Father God, You who make all things new through the power of the Holy Spirit, renew my mind, I pray! May I not conform to the things of this world, but instead may I be continually transformed by the renewing of my mind with Your Word.

Lord in many ways I have been lazy and undisciplined in regards to the use of my mind. Forgive me, I pray, and renew my mind. I lay before you my use of my computer and technology, my TV and DVD viewing, the things I read . . . (*Pause and allow the Holy Spirit to speak to you.*)

I have entertained philosophies of the world that are contrary to Your Word. Lord, forgive me and renew my mind. I lay before you the way that I have rationalized behavior or condoned values of this world . . . (*Pause and allow the Holy Spirit to speak to you.*)

I have watered down the truth of Your Word in order to condone my sin. Lord forgive me and renew my mind. I lay before you the excuses that I have made for my thoughts, attitudes, and actions that are contrary to Your Word . . . (*Pause and allow the Holy Spirit to speak to you.*)

I have allowed fear and anxious thoughts to overwhelm me. Lord, forgive me and renew my mind and make my heart steadfast. I choose now to cast all of my cares and fears onto You and ask that Your peace be poured out on me . . . (*Pause and allow the Holy Spirit to speak to you.*)

Give me, I pray, a fresh hunger to study Your Word, that I might be equipped for every good work. And Father, in a world of watered -down truth, empty philosophies, and hopelessness, empower me by Your Spirit to be prepared to answer everyone who asks me to give the reason for the hope that I have. May Jesus be seen clearly in my daily living. Strengthen my faith, Father, for Your Word says that if I do not stand firm in my faith I will not stand at all. O God, help me to stand. In Jesus' name. Amen.

Romans 12:2; Colossians 2:8; John 17:17; 2 Timothy 2:15; Philippians 4:7-8; 1 Peter 3:15; Isaiah 7:9

O Lord, You Are My Strength

Before you begin, sit quietly before the Lord. Ask to be given a "willing spirit"—willing to repent, to change, to listen, to obey.

Father, thank You for the promise of Your Word that those who hope in You will renew their strength. You alone are the source of all strength, for You are the ruler of all things and in Your hands are strength and power to exalt and give strength to me. Strengthen me to stand firm, to stand for righteousness, to stand for Your kingdom! Like Daniel, may my life be characterized by integrity and "above-reproach conduct." Even in the midst of injustice, may I be one who turns to You in worship and thanksgiving. May I always run toward You and not grow weary. Empower me, I pray, to walk and not faint. Help me to not fear or be dismayed, regardless of the situations that I am in, or the condition of the world around me—for You are God and You hold all things together. Hold me together, I pray! Strengthen me and help me—uphold me with Your righteous right hand and with power through Your Spirit in my inner being, so that Christ may dwell in my heart in all of His fullness—in *all* His fullness! Have mercy on me, Father and help me to lean on You and find my strength in You alone for my spirit is willing but my flesh is so weak and I confess to You, Lord:

the weakness of my faith and flesh . . . O Lord, have mercy!

the undisciplined use of my mind . . . Renew and strengthen my mind by Your Word!

the sin that I yet hold on to . . . Wash me and cleanse me.

the timid ways in which I still live . . . I turn from a spirit of fear and trust in Your name!

Increase my faith. Destroy doubt and unbelief in my heart and mind and empower me to live boldly. May the sphere of influence in which You've planted me resonate with the praise of Your name and the imprint of Jesus be left on all that I touch. For Your name and Your renown are the desire of my heart. In Jesus' powerful name I pray. Amen.

Isaiah 40:31; 1 Chronicles 29:12; Isaiah 41:10; Daniel 6; Isaiah 40:31; Isaiah 41:10; Colossians 1:17; Ephesians 3:16-17; 2 Corinthians 12:9-10; Matthew 26:41; Romans 12:29; Psalm 51:7; Isaiah 12:2; Isaiah 26:8

DAY SIXTEEN

The Indwelling Holy Spirit

How I thank You, Father, for the indwelling presence of the Holy Spirit. Thank You for bringing me, by the blood of the Lord Jesus, from death to life, and from being under the law to being under

Your grace. May Your great love and tenderness compel me toward greater obedience.

> I ask, Father, that You forgive me for the ways that I have allowed sin to continue to reign in my life . . .
>
> For attitudes that I have nurtured that are full of self and detrimental to my relationship with You and others . . .
>
> For focusing on the darkness of this world, instead of the light of Your presence, Lord Jesus, forgive me. May my mind and attitudes be controlled by the Spirit and produce life and peace.
>
> For actions and habits in my life that do not push me toward greater Christlikeness, forgive me, Lord. Crush the walls of excuses that I have erected that keep them so firmly in place!

O God, may Your Word dwell in me richly and may whatever I do or say be done in Your name, that You might receive glory and praise. Make me to be, I pray, a slave to righteousness and lead me toward holiness! Help me to live under the law of the Spirit, to live and move and have my very being in You alone, for I know it is Your desire that I be holy and blameless. Make me alive in Your Spirit that I might be like a tree planted by the water and never fail to bear fruit. May I live by the Spirit so that I will not gratify the desires of the sinful nature and keep in step with what the Spirit is doing. May the fruit of the Spirit be born in my life in ever-increasing measure. May love, joy, peace, patience, kindness, goodness, faithfulness, gentleness, and self-control be evident in my words, actions, and reactions. Conform me, I pray, to the image of Jesus, for I ask these things in His name. Amen.

1 Corinthians 3:16; Romans 6:13; Romans 8:6; Colossians 3:16-17; Romans 6:19; Acts 17:28; Ephesians 5:26-27; Jeremiah 17:8; Galatians 5:16, 25, 22-23

Come Out of the Shadows

Father, I'm so grateful that through Christ Jesus, the law of the Spirit of life has set me free from the law of sin and death! Thank You, Jesus, for willingly becoming my sin-offering; that my sins have been forgiven and forgotten; and that You have given me Your righteousness is beyond my ability to understand, but I am so very thankful!

And now Lord, knowing that I am Yours and that the Holy Spirit lives in me, may my mind be set on what the Spirit desires. I ask in Jesus' name that You break all residual strongholds of my sinful nature, that my mind be controlled by Your Spirit and produce life and peace in me. I choose this day to put to death the misdeeds of my body that I might truly live! Thank You for the Spirit of sonship, that I am Yours and call You "Father" is more than I can comprehend! Empower me to live as Your child. (*Pause and consider that you are a child of God!*)

How I thank You, Lord Jesus, that while I was still captive and imprisoned by my sin, You came and proclaimed freedom! Forgive me for the ways that I live as if Your sacrifice for my sin is not enough. Truly my sin is great, but Your grace is greater still, and You have given me Your robe and ring and have invited me to feast at Your table! Forgive me Father, for the ways that I think, speak, or live that are as if I am a slave in Your house, instead of Your child! Forgive me for living in the shadows.

Empower me, this day, by Your Spirit that is at work in me, to live boldly in the freedom that You have provided for me, in Christ. Transform my living and fill me with Your joy! Thank You that where the Spirit is, there is freedom. Words are inadequate to express my thanks, Lord Jesus, for destroying the curse of sin and setting me free!

Thank You for this glorious freedom! Strengthen me to come out of the shadows of my living, and walk in Your great light. In Jesus' name. Amen.

Romans 8:2-17; Galatians 5:1; Isaiah 61:1; Luke 4:18; Luke 15:11-31; 2 Corinthians 3:17; Galatians 5:13; 1 Corinthians 8:9; Romans 8:21

From the Inside Out

Father, Jesus said that I am to love You
    with all of my heart,
    with all of my mind,
    with all of my strength, and
    to love my neighbor as myself—that this is more important
        than anything else that I do.

Forgive me, Lord, for I know that I have kept parts of my heart hidden and distant from You.

I have been slothful in my thinking, lazy, and undisciplined and have not loved You with all of my mind. I'm so very aware of my weakness and confess that I am not sure that I know what loving You with all of my strength even looks like.

Father, You know that I rarely love others as much as I love myself. Forgive me, Lord.

Have mercy on me and change me O God! May my life be marked by deep heart-belief and mouth confession that Jesus is Lord. Keep me, I pray, from self-imposed, outward moral reformation that leads to joyless, disempowered living. Instead, may I be continually spiritually transformed, conformed to the character of Jesus, that the reflection of His glory may be seen in me and others will be drawn to Him. Change me from the inside out, I pray.

May I truly believe in my heart what I confess with my mouth, so that my faith will not shrivel within me when faced with the difficulties of life, or be hypocritical and harsh as I live in front of those who have yet to call on Your name.

O how I long for my heart and mind to align under Your Lordship. I am weary Lord of unbelief and double-mindedness! Save me from myself, I pray. I confess with my mouth, Lord Jesus, that You alone are Lord to the glory of God the Father. Now may it be true in my heart as well and lived out this day through my life. In the mighty name of Him who alone can accomplish these things. Amen.

Mark 12:33; 2 Corinthians 3:18; 1 Peter 3:15; Deuteronomy 30:14; Matthew 5:16; Mark 9:24; Romans 10:9-10; Philippians 2:11

DAY NINETEEN

The Imprint of Jesus

Father, I come before You this day, overwhelmed by Your holiness and greatness. In light of who You are, I am keenly aware of the weakness of my fleshly nature. Have mercy on me, O God. Forgive me for going my own way and not aligning my life with Your perfect will. I confess that I have been misguided by my own self-serving purposes and have lost sight of Your face. Remove from me, I pray, the shame of my sin that keeps me from running into Your arms, looking on Your face, and receiving Your forgiveness. I ask this day, Father, for a fresh infilling of Your Holy Spirit that will transform the way I live and display Your glory to those who do not yet know You.

This day, Father, may my mind be set on things above, not on things of this earth. May I be a person of blessing this day. Help me to encourage those who are tired and wearied by the cares of this world. Give me opportunity to love in deed and action. May I be willing to be inconvenienced for the sake of the gospel and minister to others as if I were ministering to You. Father it is my desire that the imprint of Jesus be left behind wherever I go, whatever I encounter, whoever I meet. Accomplish this through me.

Father, I do not want to be one who follows You halfheartedly or out of convenience. May I always stand firm and not allow anything to move me away from You and give myself wholly to Your purposes. How grateful I am that You are compassionate and gracious, that You know my weakness! Thank You for not treating me as my sin deserves. Restore to me, I pray, the joy of Your salvation and sustain me with a willing spirit that Your glory might be displayed through my life. These things I pray in Jesus' name. Amen.

Luke 15:20-24; Colossians 3:1; Hebrews 3:13; Hebrews 10:25; James 2:20, 26; Matthew 25:40; Matthew 5:16; 1 Corinthians 15:58; Psalm 103:8-19; Psalm 51:12-13

Fill Up What Is Lacking

Father, Your Word promises that You will be my sure foundation, a rich store of salvation and wisdom and knowledge. Forgive me Lord, for I know that I often look in other places for strength and stability and miss Your blessing in my life. Forgive me for the times that I turn to the wisdom of the world, instead of turning to You. I am so quick to take matters into my own hands and do what is right in my own eyes. Teach me to pause, to seek Your face, wisdom, and counsel. You have said in Your Word that if I lack wisdom I should ask, and so I ask, Father, give me Your wisdom, I pray.

Guard my mind today against worldly philosophies. May I be rooted firmly in Christ!

In the situations that I face at work, home, or school, may I know Your mind and be wise in all I do. Keep me from error, and I ask for Your wisdom especially in regard to . . . (*Pray through your schedule and concerns.*)

May Your wisdom be evident through me as I engage those in my life with whom I have relationships.

I declare my dependence upon You alone, the source of all knowledge and wisdom, and I ask that You give me wisdom from heaven that is:

pure (Reveal the hidden motives of my heart Father!);

peace loving (May my words build others up and promote unity, I pray.);

considerate and submissive (May my thoughts be of the needs of others—teach me to serve!);

full of mercy and good fruit (May I be a dispenser of Your great grace.);

impartial and sincere (May my actions flow out of my love
for You—help me to love like You love.)

Strengthen me today. Remind me, I pray, to live out what Your Word
says—that I might be like a wise man who builds his house on a rock, that
regardless of the storms that come against me, I might not be moved. In
the name of Jesus, who is the Word. Amen.

Isaiah 33:6; 1 Corinthians 3:19; Proverbs 3:7; Colossians 1:9; Ephesians 1:17;
James 1:5; Colossians 2:8-9; James 3:17; Matthew 7:24-25

DAY TWENTY-ONE

Teach Me the Way of Humility

**Before you begin, like the disciples in Luke 11:1, simply ask,
"Lord, teach me to pray."**

Father, I come before You asking that You empower me by Your
Spirit that the humility of Christ might be evident in my relationships with others. May I do nothing out of selfishness but truly consider
others better than myself and look out for the interests of those You have
placed in my life. Father this is so against my nature!

Forgive me Lord—for I confess that more often than not I am more
concerned with my own needs, and getting my own way. May selfishness be put to death in me that I might truly serve others in love.

Forgive me, Father, for I confess that often my involvement in the
needs of others is based on my own comfort or if it's convenient for me.
How selfish I am Lord! Teach me what it means to love sacrificially I

35

pray—to love like Jesus, to serve like Jesus! Teach me this way.

May I extend grace and mercy to others as You, Father, have extended grace and mercy to me. Destroy pride in my life in all of its ugly forms: the need to have my own way, to be heard, to be right, to be noticed and appreciated, excusing sin in my life . . . (pause and allow the Holy Spirit to speak to you). Help me to be keenly aware of the ways that I exalt myself, and may I instead exalt Christ.

Your Word promises that You will guide the humble in what is right—I want to be guided by You! I choose this day to submit to the promptings of Your Holy Spirit, to not resist His work in my life, and to humble myself under Your mighty hand that You might lift me up in due time as You see fit. May the refining fire of the Holy Spirit have full reign in my life this day that I might be a useable vessel for the purposes of Your Kingdom. And may I be an extension of Your love and mercy to those who are burdened with the cares and brokenness of this world and are in desperate need of the Savior. I ask these things in His Mighty Name. Amen.

Philippians 2:2-4; Galatians 5:13; Galatians 6:2; Daniel 4:37; Psalm 25:9; 1 Peter 5:6; Luke 10:25-37

DAY TWENTY-TWO

You Are Great, O God

O LORD, how majestic is Your name in all the earth! Your glory is above the heavens. When I look at the night sky and see the work of Your hands, the moon and the stars which You have set in place, Your greatness overwhelms me, and in my heart I feel so small and insignificant. Yet You tell me that You have made me a little lower than the angels and crowned me with glory and honor, made me ruler over the works of Your hands, and have put everything under my feet! That You, O God, creator of all things calls me by name and says "do not fear I am with you, I have redeemed you, you are mine," is a blessing too great to comprehend!

That You have called me out of the darkness of my sin and into the wonderful light of the Lord Jesus makes my heart overflow with thanksgiving! For I remember when I was still dead in my sin, hopeless and despairing, but You have rescued me from that dominion of darkness and brought me into the kingdom of Jesus and my sins have been forgiven! My slate has been wiped clean! Hallelujah! O God, purify me, I pray, that I might be found living a life that is worthy of the calling that I have received from You.

Open the eyes of my heart ever wider, I pray, that I might have a clearer understanding of the "glorious inheritance" that You have called me to. Strengthen me in my inner man that I might always press on toward You. May I press on *today*. Renew my passion and hunger to know You and to be in Your presence. Help me to live as one who has been called by the God of the universe into intimate fellowship and communion. I confess my weakness to you, the difficulty that I have almost continually, to remain steadfast and focused on Your face alone. Help me, Lord! Be strong in my weakness I pray, and accomplish all that You intend. Be glorified, Father—in me and through me. I ask this in Jesus' name. Amen.

Psalm 8; Isaiah 43:1; 1 Peter 2:9; 2 Timothy 1:9; 1 Corinthians 1:2;
1 Thessalonians 2:12; Ephesians 4:1; Ephesians 1:18; Philippians 3:14;
1 Corinthians 1:8-9; 2 Corinthians 12:9

Dead to Sin

Before you begin, ask God for a fresh outpouring of the Holy Spirit on your life.

Lord Jesus Christ, it is in Your mighty name that I pray.

Father, Your Word says that a patient man is better than a warrior and one who controls his temper than one who takes a city. You have admonished me in Your Word to control my body—my appetites and behavior—in a way that is holy and honorable to You. But I confess, Father, that I fall short of this in many areas of my life, and I ask that You strengthen me by Your Spirit, so that I might not let sin reign in my body or give in to evil desires (*Pause and ask the Holy Spirit to reveal those areas of your life that are not yet submitted to Him.*)

May the fruit of self-control continually increase in my life that this godly characteristic may be evident in the way that I eat, how I shop, the hobbies I engage in, my sexuality, my words and actions. . . . May every aspect of who I am and how I live be under the control of the Holy Spirit. I submit to You now in Jesus' name, Father.

Empower me to keep a tight rein on my tongue. May I be quick to listen, slow to speak, and slow to become angry, knowing that anger does not bring about the righteous life that You desire. May I bless with my mouth and my life.

May my life be so controlled by Your Holy Spirit that I truly live and move and have my very being in You alone. Help me this day to not indulge my fleshly nature. Strengthen me to stand firm and be self-controlled in thought, word, and action—that I might be a usable, noble vessel for Your purposes and the glory of Your great

name. Accomplish this through Christ in me, for I pray in His name.
Amen.

Proverbs 16:32; 1 Thessalonians 4:4; Romans 6:12; 2 Peter 1:5-6; Daniel 1:8; 1 Corinthians 6:19; James 1:26; James 1:19; Acts 17:28; Romans 9:21

Father, You Are Faithful

Before you begin, ask the Holy Spirit to quiet your heart and bring to your mind the many reasons you have to be thankful. Spend time recounting the goodness of the Lord.

Father, it is good to praise You and proclaim Your love in the morning and Your faithfulness at night. You are the One who makes me glad! Open my eyes to see the works of Your hands and sponsor in me, by Your Spirit, songs of joy, for You are worthy of the highest praise I can offer!

Forgive me, Father, for allowing my heart to be captured by the cares of this world instead of You and Your greatness. Like Paul and Silas, may I be found singing in the "prisons" that I face! How thankful I am for the sacrifice of Jesus for my sin, that He has saved me completely and intercedes for me! Hallelujah! What a great salvation is mine! Lord, You are great and awesome!

May I always sing of Your great love and make known with my mouth Your continuing faithfulness through all generations. For Your love stands firm forever—Your faithfulness stands firm in heaven itself. And I know that You are able to do above and beyond anything that I can even imagine. Help me to always enter into Your presence with thanksgiving and praise, for You are good and Your love endures forever.

Thank You, Father, for reaching down and taking hold of me, for rescuing me, and being my support in days of trouble. That You delight in me is beyond my ability to grasp. Help me Lord to hear the song that You sing over me. Satisfy me this morning with Your unfailing love, that I may sing for joy and be glad all day. May Your favor rest upon me, Lord. I ask that You establish the work of my hands this day, and may kingdom purposes be accomplished in and through my life for my hope is in You, the maker of heaven and earth. You are my great reward, and I praise Your holy name.

Psalm 92:1-4; Acts 16:25; Hebrews 7:25, 27; Psalm 89:1-2; Ephesians 3:20; Psalm 100:4-5; Psalm 18:16-19; Zephaniah 3:17; Psalm 90:17; Psalm 115:15; Genesis 15:1

DAY TWENTY-FIVE

Teach Me to Pray

Thank You, Father, that Jesus has borne my sin and intercedes for me, that because of His blood, shed for me, I have confidence to enter into Your most holy Presence. I want to draw near to You with a sincere heart in full assurance that as I call on You, You will answer me and show me great and unsearchable things that I do not know.

Teach me to pray, O God! Teach me to pray Your heart, Your will, Your Word. Forgive me, Lord, for I am often self-focused in Your presence and give in to the worries of this life and miss the blessing of praying Your heart for your Church and the world around me. Empower me by Your Spirit to intercede for others and Your work around the world. May I become one that You call on, even in the watches of the night, to "build up the wall" and stand in the gap on behalf of others—and may I respond when You call. May the burden and intensity of the needs of a lost world, my brothers and sisters in Christ, and my community of faith so overtake me, that I cannot keep silent day or night before You. Make me to be a watchman for Your Kingdom, Father!

Like Anna, may I never leave Your presence but learn to worship, fast, and pray continually. Teach me what it means to be persistent in prayer until I receive the answer, to always pray and never give up. Help me to rise before dawn and cry out to You, always putting my hope in the promises of Your Word. May Your Word be in my heart like a burning fire and Your promises, my constant meditation. Mold me, Father, into a prayer warrior for Your Kingdom. Teach me to pray in Your Spirit that I might become one who is truly devoted to prayer and who participates with You in Your work, even to the ends of the earth! May prayer truly become the foundation of my living that I might be one who is found faithful, always praying—refusing to give up. In Jesus' name. Amen.

Isaiah 53:12; Hebrews 10:19-20; Jeremiah 33:3; Matthew 6:25-33; Ezekiel 22:30; Isaiah 62:6-7; Ezekiel 3:17; Luke 2:37; Luke 11:5-9; Psalm 119:147; Jeremiah 23:29; Psalm 1:2; Colossians 4:2; Luke 18:1-6

Resurrection Life

Lord Jesus, You said that You are the resurrection and the life, and that if anyone believes in You, they too will live! Jesus, I believe! You are the Christ, the Son of the living God, the Savior of the world, who was raised from the dead, has gone into heaven, and is at God's right hand—with angels, authorities, and powers in submission to You! I want to truly know You, Lord Jesus, and the power of Your resurrection in my life. Show me what this means and teach me by Your Spirit, for I cannot comprehend the magnitude of this! In light of this resurrection power I ask you to change the way that I live. Transform me, I pray, that my life may be characterized by ever-increasing boldness and confidence in You—for my Savior lives! By Your Spirit, empower me to live above the circumstances and daily situations that surround me, for I know that I have been raised with You through my faith in the power of God the Father Who raised You from the dead.

How grateful I am that I have been made alive with You! Thank You for forgiving me all of my sins and canceling the written law, with its regulations, that was against me—that stood opposed to me. Thank You for taking it away and nailing it to the cross. Thank You, Jesus, for disarming the powers of darkness and making a public spectacle of them by triumphing over them by the cross! How I praise God that You have been raised from the dead! For I know that if You had not been raised, my faith would be futile. Lord Jesus, I believe that You died and rose again and because of this, I know that You will come again—that You will come down from heaven, with a loud command, with the voice of the archangel, and with the trumpet call of God the Father, and those who have died in You will rise first. After that, if I am still alive on the earth, I will be caught up, with my brothers and sisters in Christ, in the clouds to meet You in the air, and will be with You forever. Hallelujah! What a Savior! Even so, come quickly Lord Jesus!

John 11:35; Matthew 16:16; 1 John 4:14; 1 Peter 3:21-22; Philippians 3:10; Colossians 2:12-15; 1 Corinthians 15:12, 17

DAY TWENTY-SEVEN

Reveal the Hidden Things

Quiet your heart before the Lord and meditate on the cross and the incredible sacrifice of Jesus on your behalf.

Thank You, Lord Jesus, for bearing my sin in Your body on the cross so that I might die to sin and live for righteousness. Thank You for the provision of healing found in Your great sacrifice. Forgive me, I pray, for the times I treat casually the freedom I have in You, do not live for righteousness, and allow myself to become enslaved again in the yoke of sin. Have mercy on me, Lord, and heal me, for I know I have sinned against You.

By Your Spirit, teach me what it means to "live for righteousness," to "seek righteousness," that You, Jesus, may be seen in me more and more, and that lasting spiritual fruit may be born out of my life. Keep me from outwardly drawing near to You with words and actions and yet keeping my heart closed off to You.

I ask, Lord Jesus, that You open every closed chamber of my heart—places I am even unaware of—and expose them by the light of Your Spirit. Remove every cobweb. You alone can heal the broken and wounded places of my heart. Where I am blind to my own sin, restore my sight, I pray. Where the enemy is oppressing me and holding me back from deeper relationship with You, release me Lord! I ask that You, my Healer, grant me complete freedom in areas of my life that have not yet been captured by Your great love. (*Pause and ask the Holy Spirit to reveal the hidden things of your heart to you.*) Only You can bring healing to the hidden places of my heart, and I invite You, Holy Spirit, to change me until I am conformed to the image of Christ.

Destroy pride in me and everything that holds me back from sharing my pilgrimage with my brothers and sisters in Christ, from confessing my sins and finding healing. I praise You, Lord, for You are the One that heals me! And I trust in You for healing of my body, mind, and soul. These things I pray with confidence, Lord Jesus, because of Your finished work on the cross. Amen.

---

1 Peter 2:24; Galatians 5:1; Psalm 41:4; John 15:16; Isaiah 29:13; Psalm 147:3; Zephaniah 2:3; 1 Peter 2:24; Romans 8:29; James 5:16; Exodus 15:26

DAY TWENTY-EIGHT

Teach Me to Love

Father, You who are the author of love; teach me Your way. I know, Father, that so often I do not love as You have called me to love. I love when it is convenient, when I'm in the right mood, or even worse, only if someone has been loving to me. Forgive me. Have mercy on me, Lord. Forgive my self-serving, selfish loving. Fill me with Your love and compassion.

You have said that love is patient and kind, it does not envy or boast, it isn't arrogant or rude, selfish, or easily provoked. It does not keep record of wrong or rejoice in unrighteousness. Father, give me this kind of love for those around me! May my love for my family members, my co-workers, and neighbors—my brothers and sisters in Christ Jesus—truly bear all things, believe all things, hope all things, and endure all things. Keep my love from failing. May I practice lavish love with them, so that I may live out Your love in the world that has yet to know You.

May extravagant love be evident in my relationships with my brothers and sisters in Jesus. Keep me from having any part in that which would cause division in the body of Christ. Instead, may my life be rooted and established in love. Father, Your Word says that it is by the way that I love those in my community of faith that the world will know that I belong to You. Give me this kind of love, I pray! As You have lavishly loved me, may I in turn love others and encourage my brothers and sisters in Christ Jesus on toward even greater love and good deeds. May I be found worthy of bearing the name of Christ and determined to live out the debt of love I owe so that Jesus may be exalted, His name glorified, and the transforming power of His love made evident in my life. In His name, I ask these things. Amen.

---

1 John 4:16; Matthew 5:38-48; 1 Corinthians 13:4-8; 1 Corinthians 12:25-27; John 13:34-35; Ephesians 3:17; 1 John 3:1; Hebrews 10:24; Romans 13:8-10

DAY TWENTY-NINE

I Wait on You, O Lord

How thankful I am, Father, that You are patient with me, slow to anger, and abounding in love. Forgive me for not treating others with the same gentle patience that You have shown me. (*Pause and pray for those you find difficult to love.*) Empower me, I pray, by Your Spirit, to be patient with everyone.

Forgive me for the many ways I impatiently run out ahead of You and do things in my own strength. Teach me to wait on You and to walk in the way of Your Word as I do so. May Your name and renown be the desire of my heart in every situation that I face in my daily pilgrimage. Strengthen me to be patient in affliction and to persevere so that I may be mature and complete, not lacking anything. I confess that I cannot do this in my own strength and ask that you empower me according to Your glorious might so that I might have great endurance and patience.

Father, may I be one who waits patiently as I hope for what I do not yet see in the circumstances and relationships of my life, knowing that all who wait for You are blessed. May I be patient and stand firm in my faith, for surely Jesus is coming soon! As I wait for His glorious appearing, may my life be characterized by patient hope and endurance. For I know the day will come when I, along with all Your people, will declare: "Surely this is our God, we trusted in Him and He saved us. This is the LORD, we trusted in Him, let us rejoice and be glad!" May I be one who imitates those who through faith and patience inherited what had been promised. And so this day, Father, I choose to wait for You, to trust in You, to hope in You, knowing that those who hope in You are not disappointed. Strengthen me to stand. I pray in Jesus' name. Amen.

---

2 Peter 3:9; Psalm 86:15; Isaiah 26:8; Romans 12:12; James 1:4; Colossians 1:11; Romans 8:25; Isaiah 30:18; James 5:8; Isaiah 25:9; Hebrews 6:12; Psalm 22:5

Find Me Faithful Lord

Lord Jesus Christ, it is in Your name that I pray . . .

Father, how very thankful I am that Your faithfulness endures forever, that even though my journey with You is often marked by my faithlessness and unbelief, You remain faithful, for You cannot deny Yourself. How great is Your faithfulness! Forgive me, I pray, for I often look away from Your greatness, lose sight of Your face, and throw away my confidence in You.

Strengthen me by Your Spirit so that I am able to persevere, do Your will, and receive what has been promised. For I know that in just a little while Jesus is coming, and You have called me to live by faith. I do not want to be one who puts his hand to the plow and then turns back! Help me to faithfully follow hard after You and walk in the light of Your presence. May my heart be set on pilgrimage with You alone, and like Moses, may I be faithful as a servant in Your house and work as faithfully as those who built the temple, in order to see Your purposes prevail and Jesus exalted! For You have given to me a sacred trust, the message of reconciliation through Jesus Christ, and You have required that I be found faithful.

Father, You know my weakness and weariness and the temptations of this world that pull at my heart and encourage me to wander. Strengthen me, I pray! Pour out Your Holy Spirit on me this day that I might faithfully follow hard after You and become, more and more, one who is sure of what I yet hope for and certain of what I do not yet see. (*Pause and commit to the Lord again, those things that you are still waiting for.*)

Do all of this, I pray, that on that glorious day when I see Your face I might hear You say, "Well done, good and faithful servant." In Jesus' mighty name I pray. Amen.

Psalm 117:2; 2 Timothy 2:13; Lamentations 3:23; Hebrews 10:35-38; Luke 9:62; Psalm 89:15; Psalm 84:5; Hebrews 3:5; 2 Chronicles 34:12; 2 Corinthians 5:18; 1 Corinthians 4:2; Hebrews 11:1; Matthew 25:21

DAY THIRTY-ONE

May Your Kingdom Come in Me

Father in heaven, how great is Your name! How awesome and unsearchable are your deeds! It is You who formed the mountains and created the wind. You turn dawn to darkness and tread the high places of the earth—the LORD God Almighty is Your name! There is none like You and I praise Your awesome name! May Your will be accomplished on earth, O God—in my life, Lord. I submit to You and Your will and ask that as it is in heaven—where saints and angels worship and adore You and there is perfect unity—may it be so here as well. May Your kingdom come Lord!

I confess my great need of You more than anything else, Father. Be my daily bread, I pray. I want to feast on You until all other desires fade, my love of the world is destroyed, and my heart is stayed on You alone. Satisfy me, Father, with Your great love and forgive me, I pray, for sinning against You. I confess that too often my thoughts, words, and actions are not Christlike and do not honor You. Instead of reaching out to others with the love of Jesus, I shrink back. Instead of blessing, encouraging, and edifying others, I keep silent. Even in sharing

Your goodness and proclaiming Your greatness I have kept quiet. O God, have mercy on me!

Destroy my self-focused living and change me by the power of the Spirit at work in me, I pray. May I be quick to forgive others, always remembering the great debt that has been forgiven me. I confess this day that Yours alone is the kingdom and the power and the glory forever and ever. You alone are able to do above and beyond anything that I can think or imagine. I proclaim with all of heaven, "Great and marvelous are your deeds Lord God Almighty. Just and true are Your ways, King of the ages. Who will not fear You, O Lord, and bring glory to Your name? For You alone are holy!" Hallelujah! Praise never ending be to You, O God! In the name of Jesus, the Christ, the Son of the only true God, I pray. Amen and amen.

Psalm 65:5; Amos 4:13; Psalm 99:3; 1 John 2:15-17; Psalm 51:4; Luke 19:37-40; Matthew 6:12-15; Ephesians 3:20; Revelation 15:3-4

Appendix

Putting on the Armor of God

Father, today I acknowledge that every battle in my life is not mine, but belongs to You. For I know that my real struggle is not against what I can see with my eyes, but with what is unseen—the powers of this dark world, the devil who waits for an opportune moment to steal, kill, and destroy Your work in my life, to ensnare me.

Father, forgive me, for I have not been self-controlled and alert. I've allowed myself to be lulled into complacency by the noise and distractions of the world. I have not resisted the enemy. Most of the time at best, I pretend he does not exist. But Your Word admonishes me to stand firm in my faith, that if I do not, I will not stand at all. Lord, teach me to stand.

Today, as You have instructed me, I choose to put on Your full armor so that I might stand against the devil's schemes and stand my ground when the day of evil comes upon me. I pray that I might be strong in You and Your mighty power! I choose to "put on" Jesus!

I stand firm then with the belt of truth buckled securely around my waist. Jesus, You are the way and the truth and the life . . . I turn from all false teaching and philosophies of this world, and I put on Jesus, the Truth.

I put on the breastplate of righteousness. Jesus, there was no sin found in You, yet You took my sin on Yourself so that I might become the righteousness of God! This day, I turn from all sin that entangles me and holds me back, and I put on Jesus, my righteousness.

I choose today to fit my feet with readiness that comes from the gospel of peace. Lord Jesus, You are my peace, for You have destroyed the barrier that was between me and God the Father! Make me ready to give the reason for the hope that I have, for I long to share with others that You, Lord Jesus, are my peace!

I take up this day the shield of faith so that I might be able to extinguish all the flaming arrows—the attacks of the evil one. The life I live in this mortal body, I live by faith in You, the Son of God, who loved me and who gave Yourself for me. May my faith in You increase as I hear Your Word and put it into practice—for You, Lord Jesus, are the author and perfecter of my faith.

I put on the helmet of salvation and declare that salvation is found in no one else, for there is no other name under heaven by which I can be saved from my sin! You, Lord Jesus, are the Christ, the Son of the Living God! Jesus, You are my salvation!

I take up this day the sword of the Spirit, which is the Word of God, and I proclaim Lord Jesus that You are the Word made flesh. You will accomplish all that You intend! Hallelujah!

Father, I choose today to clothe myself with Christ, to be alert and ready to pray—to pray in the Spirit no matter the occasion or situation that I am in, with all kinds of prayers and requests. May I become one who is increasingly faithful in prayer.

In all of these things, I put on Christ Jesus—and I take my stand! May Your power that is at work in me this day, be mighty. I ask all these things in the name of Jesus, who gave Himself for me that I might truly live. Amen and Amen.

2 Chronicles 20:15; John 10:10; 1 Peter 5:8-9; Isaiah 7:9; Ephesians 6:10-13; Ephesians 6:14; John 14:6; Colossians 2:8; Ephesians 6:14; Philippians 3:8-16; Hebrews 12:1; Ephesians 6:15; Ephesians 2:13-18; Ephesians 6:16; Galatians 2:20; Romans 10:17; James 1:22-25; Ephesians 6:17; Acts 4:12; Matthew 16:16; Ephesians 6:17; John 1:14; Isaiah 55:11; Ephesians 6:18; Romans 12:12

Scripture Prayers for the Body of Christ

Personalize the following prayers for your community of faith.

As We Worship

Father, prepare the hearts of Your people to worship You as we gather. Prepare my heart, I pray! May each of us come before You with songs of thanksgiving and joy! Pour out Your Spirit on us as we gather.

Father I ask that You build Your house—we do not want to labor in vain! In Your good pleasure, make Your church prosper. May many be led to Jesus and Your love spread through the city through our lives. May Your favor rest upon us, Lord. Establish the work of our hands.

You are the God of all hope, Father. I pray that You will fill my brothers and sisters in Christ with joy and peace that their hearts might overflow with hope through the power of the Holy Spirit. Where there is depression or despair, discouragement or doubt, may it be dispelled in Jesus' name and the encouragement of the Holy Spirit be poured out on their lives.

May our times of personal and corporate worship be infused with fresh Spirit-life, I pray. May we worship You in spirit and in truth and give You the glory due Your name.

Reveal to us in what ways we come near to You with our lips (what we say or sing in Your presence), but keep our hearts far from You.

You have said, Lord, that You will give the Holy Spirit to those who ask. Father, I ask! Fill me afresh with Your Holy Spirit! Pour out Your Spirit on my brothers and sisters in Christ at _____. Revive us. Change us! Conform us to the image of Jesus! I pray this in Jesus' name. Amen.

Ephesians 6:18; Romans 12:12; Psalm 127:1; Psalm 51:18; Psalm 90:17; Romans 15:13; John 4:23-24; Isaiah 29:13; Matthew 15:8; Luke 11:11-13; Psalm 85:6; Romans 8:29

Prayer for Others

Father, I pray for those among our community of faith who are new in their journey with You—increase their faith, Father. May they be built up, edified and encouraged. Add to our fellowship daily those who are being saved!

Father pour out the gifts of the Spirit and strengthen us as Your people to serve. May there be no lack in any area of ministry, but may we increasingly use the gifts that You have given us to serve one another. May our zeal in serving You never diminish. Strengthen those among us who have grown weary in doing what is good. Encourage them I pray.

Father, You are our healer, and I come to You on behalf of my brothers and sisters in Christ Jesus who are suffering physically. May Your healing power be poured out on them, I pray. Strengthen and renew them and may all sickness be gone in Jesus' name. I pray especially for . . . (*Pray for those you know of by name.*)

Father, I lift up to You those in our fellowship who are struggling with doubt and unbelief, and I ask in Jesus' name that the enemy be pushed back. Strengthen them to fix their eyes on Jesus and give to them, I pray, fresh faith and signs of Your goodness, so that they do not turn back.

Fill us with fresh passion for You and a hunger for holiness, that we would truly become those who seek first Your kingdom and Your righteousness. Reveal to us, I pray, the things that keep us from truly drawing near to You. Amen and Amen!

John 6:44; Acts 2:47; Romans 12:10-11; Galatians 6:9; Hebrews 12:2; Mark 9:24; Psalm 119:2; Matthew 6:33

Prayer for Our Relationships

As a community of faith, may we increasingly be those who bless with our mouths, who seek and pursue peace with one another. May we love as brothers and be compassionate and humble toward one another.

Father, I ask that Your Word would dwell in us richly, that we would overflow with Your Word. I pray, Father, that Your Word will become our only standard for our lives. Destroy the excuses that we give for our sin and conform us to the image of Jesus!

Father, You have said that the sacrifices that You are looking for are a broken spirit and contrite heart. Destroy pride among us, Lord, and give to us the gift of repentance, I pray.

Be exalted, be glorified in our conversations, in the choices that we make, and the places we go. Whether we eat or drink or whatever it is that we might do, may we always be mindful that we belong to You, and do it all for Your glory.

Father, I pray that we will become the kind of worshipers that You are seeking, those who worship in spirit and in truth. Open the eyes of our hearts and reveal the hidden things, for You have said that You desire truth in our inmost parts. Show us, Lord, show me, where I am still withholding my heart from You.

I pray for my brothers and sisters and ask that we might all "run the race" in such a way as to be found worthy of the prize. May our daily living display Christ in greater and greater clarity and the imprint of Jesus left in our wake.

I ask in Jesus' mighty name that every stronghold of addiction be broken off of us as Your people. Reveal the hidden things, Father! Purify us and make us holy! In Jesus' name, Amen!

---

1 Peter 3:8-12; Colossians 3:16; Colossians 1:19-20; Psalm 51:16-17; 1 Corinthians 10:31; John 4:23-24; Ephesians 1:18; Job 28:11; Psalm 51:6; 1 Corinthians 9:27; Job 28:11

Bearing Spiritual Fruit

Give us "God-sized" dreams for the ministries that you wish to accomplish through us. Forgive our lack of faith and embolden us to be risk takers for the sake of Your kingdom!

Lord Jesus, help us to abide in You that we as Your people might bear spiritual fruit that will last and, by doing so, show that we are truly Your disciples.

Allow us, I pray, to see harvest come in and souls come to know Jesus! Father I pray for pre-Christian friends, co-workers, family members, who are connected to our community of faith—Lord Jesus, may their longing for You increase. Make us ready to give the reason for the hope that we have in You. (*Pray for those in your life who do not yet know Jesus by name.*)

Father, protect us from the love of money. May we be increasingly content with what we have, knowing that You will never leave us.

Renew our minds, I pray. May we as Your people turn from the philosophies and entertainment of the world and truly think on things that are true, noble, right, pure, lovely, admirable, excellent, and praiseworthy—may this be the standard for what we allow into our minds and hearts.

May we, from youngest to oldest, become those who do not just hear the Word, but become those who do what it says. May we be increasingly quick and willing to obey.

Father, I pray for my brothers and sisters who are struggling with depression, anxiety, and fear. I ask that they will be strengthened by the Holy Spirit to take every thought captive and make it obedient to Christ. Destroy every stronghold. Set captives free! I pray this in Jesus' mighty name. Amen.

Hebrews 11:1, 6; John 15:5-8; 1 Peter 3:15; Hebrews 13:5-6; Philippians 4:8; James 1:22; 2 Corinthians 10:5

Bring Revival, Lord

Father, may the world know that we belong to You by the way that we love one another. May the unity of the Spirit and the bond of peace increase in our fellowship. Help us to be completely humble and gentle with one another and to bear with one another in love.

Father, You have promised to bestow on Your people the oil of gladness in place of the "ash piles" of our lives. Many of us struggle under the memories of past hurt, abuse, and loss. Heal our damaged emotions, Father. Restore joy and gladness to us, I pray!

Lord Jesus, You said that Your house was to be a "house of prayer for all nations." And so I ask that our community of faith learn the discipline of prayer. May we determine to increasingly become those who "cast every care" onto You; who "watch on the wall" for Your church; and who "always pray and never give up" until we see lives transformed, revival fall, and the last great harvest come in!

Father, I ask that You breathe new Spirit-life into our community of faith. May revival visitations of the Holy Spirit fall on us, change us, renew us, I pray! May we not resist the Holy Spirit in any way. In Jesus' name. Amen.

Ephesians 4:2-3; Isaiah 61:3; Mark 11:17; 1 Peter 5:7; Isaiah 62:6-7; Luke 18:1-8; Ezekiel 37:5

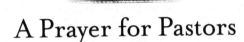

A Prayer for Pastors

Pray for your pastor(s) by name using the following prayer.

Father, bless my pastor with rest on every side. Guard his heart and mind and cloak him in Your peace. Clear the way today for him to carry out Your plans for our faith community with no interference from the enemy. I stand in prayer for him and ask in Jesus' name that the forces of darkness that would come against him be pushed back and by faith I take hold of the harvest that your Spirit is bringing forth for the kingdom of heaven through our faith community. Thank you, Lord, that each time the enemy comes in like a flood, Your Spirit will lift up a standard against him and put him to flight! I thank You for total victory for my pastor and for my church and I ask You, Lord Jesus, to meet his every need. Thank You that You are mighty to save and able to overcome and defeat every attempt of the enemy that might tempt him to lose heart! Hallelujah!

Give my pastor endurance and encouragement and clear guidance by Your Spirit for every decision required of him. May the anointing of the Holy Spirit be upon him. Revive his heart with Your Word, Father. May his love for You increase and compassion and love for his flock flourish and grow. Strengthen him with Your joy this day and may he be encouraged by the Holy Spirit and reminded of the spiritual sons and daughters that are his.

Give him wisdom that is from heaven, I pray—wisdom that is pure, peace loving, considerate, submissive, full of mercy and good fruit, impartial, and sincere. Protect him from the evil one and from being entrapped by the fear of man. Pour out Your blessing on him, Father, and may Jesus be seen in him more and more, and the work of his hands firmly established. I ask these things in the name of Him who is head of the Church, and I give You thanks, Lord Jesus, for my pastor. Amen.

---

2 Samuel 7:1; Luke 10:19; Isaiah 59:19; Psalm 44:5; James 3:17; Matthew 6:13; Proverbs 29:25; Psalm 90:17

Prayers for Your Neighborhood, City, and Nation

Exalt Jesus over Cities and Nations

Father, I declare Your Word over the city of _____. The earth is Yours, and everything in it, the world and all who live in it belong to You! Name of Nation belongs to You, Father! The city of _____ is Yours Father! And all people are Your inheritance!

This day I pray that Your Name will be exalted in this nation. Pour out Your Holy Spirit and reveal Yourself to the hearts of the people of this country through dreams and visions and through Your Church. Use us, I pray, use me, as a conduit of Your great love and compassion.

May the love of Jesus be evident in my every word, in my countenance, and in my actions. Fill me afresh with Your Holy Spirit, I pray. Empower me to be salt and light in the midst of darkness. Lord Jesus, may You be exalted in this land! May You be glorified in this nation! For You are the Christ, the Son of the Living God—there is no other God besides You, and I ask these things in the mighty name of the Lord Jesus Christ. Amen

Psalm 24:1; Joel 2:28-29; Luke 11:15; Matthew 5:13-14; Matthew 16:16; Jeremiah 10:10

Spread the Fragrance of Christ

O God, You who holds all things together and the nations in Your hand. You who in Your sovereignty have placed me here, in <u>city, nation</u>, at this time in history, and whose plans and ways are perfect, I submit to You.

Your will is that none should perish, but that all should come to repentance. In accordance with Your will, I ask that this would be so among us. May we, the church, grow through new believers. May the gospel be presented to the lost among us with power, the Holy Spirit, and deep conviction, not only through words but by our very lives. Teach us, teach me, to make the most of every opportunity that we might constantly spread everywhere the fragrance of Christ. And allow us, I pray, allow me, to be part of end-time harvest, that Jesus, the Lamb, might receive the reward for His suffering. I ask all of this in His mighty name. Amen.

Psalm 24:1; Colossians 1:17; Isaiah 46:11; James 4:7; 2 Peter 3:9; Acts 2:47; 1 Thessalonians 1:5; Colossians 4:5; 2 Corinthians 2:15

Blessings Where You Live

Father, I praise and thank You for placing me here, in this neighborhood, on this street, in this apartment/house. I acknowledge that Your plans and purposes for me are perfect and that You have placed me here that I might participate in Your plan for this neighborhood. Open my eyes to see where You are at work and help me to eagerly enter in, I pray. May Jesus be seen in me, the very light of His presence, in the way I acknowledge and greet others and reach out to those around me. Father, may the presence and power of the Holy Spirit be poured out on my dwelling place, drawing those around me to Yourself. Open the eyes of the hearts of those I encounter and make them hungry to know You. I pray Your blessing over <u>name the street where you live</u> and over the places where I purchase goods and food. Open blind eyes! Set captives free! May Jesus be revealed to the hearts of those all around me, and I lift up those I know by name. . . . Help me to minister Your love and compassion to all that I encounter. Use me, I pray, that my life might be woven into the grand tapestry of Your perfect plan for my neighborhood and this city! In Jesus' name. Amen.

Psalm 33:10-11; Psalm 139:16; Psalm 25:12-13; Psalm 107:10-16; Psalm 18:28; Ephesians 1:18; 2 Corinthians 4:4; 1 John 3:18; 1 John 4:7-12

Stay
Connected
with
Pray the Word

If you were blessed by these prayers, we invite you to connect with Pray the Word through our website and social network pages.

praytheword.net

- Find additional prayers to download--in multiple languages.
- Find other helps to encourage you in your desire to pray the Word.
- Sign up for updates on resources.

Connect with Us on Facebook
facebook.com/praytheword

- Be reminded regularly to pray the Word.
- Interact with others who are praying the Word.
- Be the first to know of new prayers that are available
- Post your own scripture-based prayers

Pray the Word is sponsored by Harvest Prayer Ministries (harvestprayer.com).

RESOURCES
Available from Pray the Word

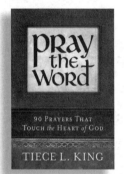

Pray the Word:
90 Prayers That Touch the Heart of God

Includes 90 powerful prayers that can move your prayer life from a fix-it focus to one that desires and surrenders to the purposes of God. Each prayer also includes space to journal either what God is saying to you or to write out additional requests the prayers stimulate in you. (Note: The first 30 prayers in this book are also included in *Pray the Word: 31 Prayers That Touch the Heart of God.*)

Available from your local Christian bookstore and prayershop.org.

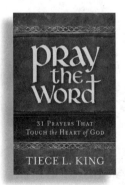

Pray the Word:
31 Prayers That Touch the Heart of God

Includes a month of scripture-based prayers that will take your prayer life to a deeper level. These prayers are not focused on our daily needs or problems, but will move us to surrender to the desires the Father has for us.

Available from your local Christian bookstore and prayershop.org.

If purchasing a quantity for your friends or church, go to prayershop.org, which has deep discounts on multiple copies.

Get the *Pray the Word* App

One month of *Pray the Word* is available as a free App for Apple and Android smartphones. The prayers are available in English, Spanish, Chinese, Indonesian, Thai, and Japanese with more languages being added as they become available. Enjoy the convenience of praying whenever you felt led to do so.

Go to the App store on your phone and search for "Pray the Word."

Coming Soon:

Pray the Word Weekly Prayer Guide

A resource especially designed for churches to disciple their people in prayer on an ongoing basis, the *Pray the Word Weekly Prayer Guide* should become available in late Spring 2014. This product is a weekly prayer guide that includes one longer scripture prayer and then a short one for each day of the week. Each week's guide is available as a pdf or Word file of an 8.5 x 11 sheet, which folds into a 4-page 5.5 x 8.5 booklet. You print out enough copies to insert in your bulletins. The Word file allows you to add some of your own special prayer needs.

This resource is available as a "Recurring Billing" subscription product. When you purchase it, your credit card will be charged each month. That gives you access to the next month's files. You can stop the arrangement at any time.

This product is available at prayershop.org.

800-217-5200 | 812-238-5504
www.prayershop.org

PRAYERSHOP
PUBLISHING

PRAYERCONNECT

Connecting to the Heart of Christ through Prayer

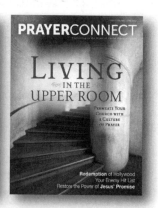

A NEW BIMONTHLY MAGAZINE DESIGNED TO:

Equip prayer leaders and pastors with tools to disciple their congregations.

Connect intercessors with the growing worldwide prayer movement.

Mobilize believers to pray God's purposes for their church, city and the nations.

Each issue of *Prayer Connect* includes:
- Practical articles to equip and inspire your prayer life.
- Helpful prayer tips and proven ideas.
- News of prayer movements around the world.
- Theme articles exploring important prayer topics.
- Connections to prayer resources available online.

Print subscription: $24.99
(includes digital version)

Digital subscription: $19.99

Church Prayer Leaders Network membership: $30 (includes print, digital, and CPLN membership benefits)

Subscribe now.
Order at www.prayerconnect.net or call 800–217–5200.